At Issue

Should the Federal Income Tax Be Eliminated?

Other Books in the At Issue Series:

At Issue

Should the Federal Income Tax Be Eliminated?

David Haugen, Book Editor

GREENHAVEN PRESS
A part of Gale, Cengage Learning

GALE
CENGAGE Learning·

Detroit • New York • San Francisco • New Haven, Conn • Waterville, Maine • London

Elizabeth Des Chenes, *Director, Content Strategy*
Cynthia Sanner, *Publisher*
Douglas Dentino, Manager, *New Product*

For more information, contact:
Greenhaven Press
27500 Drake Rd.
Farmington Hills, MI 48331-3535
Or you can visit our Internet site at gale.cengage.com

For product information and technology assistance, contact us at

Gale Customer Support, 1-800-877-4253
For permission to use material from this text or product, submit all requests online at www.cengage.com/permissions

Further permissions questions can be e-mailed to permissionrequest@cengage.com

Articles in Greenhaven Press anthologies are often edited for length to meet page requirements. In addition, original titles of these works are changed to clearly present the main thesis and to explicitly indicate the author's opinion. Every effort is made to ensure that Greenhaven Press accurately reflects the original intent of the authors. Every effort has been made to trace the owners of copyrighted material.

Cover image © Images.com/Corbis.

LIBRARY OF CONGRESS CATALOGING-IN-PUBLICATION DATA

Should the federal income tax be eliminated? / David Haugen, Book Editor.
     pages cm. -- (At issue)
   Includes bibliographical references and index.
   ISBN 978-0-7377-6201-3 (hardcover) -- ISBN 978-0-7377-6202-0 (pbk.)
   1. Income tax--United States--Juvenile literature. 2. Flat-rate income tax--United States--Juvenile literature. I. Haugen, David M., 1969-
   HJ4652.S465 2014
   336.24'150973--dc23
                                                        2013037281

Contents

Introduction

Every April 15th, most Americans grumble about paying their income taxes. Income taxes, like all taxes, have never been popular and have been the subject of derision by those forced to pay them. Such antipathy among Americans may have strong roots. The United States was born as a result of tax protests. In the mid-1700s, the early colonists resisted the notion that they should be taxed by England without their input or consent, a disagreement that eventually resulted in the American Revolution. Roughly a century later, the US government would impose its first income tax. To finance the Civil War, the government instituted a tax on income in 1861. Fearing it would be an unpopular move, Secretary of the Treasury Salmon Chase and Thaddeus Stevens, chairman of the House Ways and Means Committee, initially hoped to raise funds through a property tax, and when that idea was dropped, they imposed a modest income tax of 3 percent on yearly earnings over $800, which exempted most workers.

The following year, the government passed the Internal Revenue Act of 1862, which brought the minimum taxable income down to $600. It also added another gradation, levying 5 percent on those earning over $10,000 a year. Of the law, Stevens proclaimed, "While the rich and the thrifty will be obliged to contribute largely from the abundance of their means ... no burdens have been imposed on the industrious laborer and mechanic.... The food of the poor is untaxed; and no one will be affected by the provisions of this bill whose living depends solely on his manual labor." Even with such strong statements, the laws were quickly emended to increase revenue. In 1864, as the war dragged on and its costs rose, the government changed the tax rate to 5 percent for people earning between $600 and $5,000. Incomes between $5,000 and $10,000 were hit with a 7.5 percent tax. Still, even as legislators debated the merits of graduated income taxes, nine out of ten Americans still paid nothing because their earnings were below the threshold. Tax rates were reduced after the war, and legislators were content to see the law lapse in 1872, affirming that such action was only a temporary war measure.

Two decades later, another income tax was adopted as part of the Tariff Act of 1894. Though ostensibly inaugurated to raise revenues during a severe economic depression, many saw the act (which levied a 2 percent tax on incomes over $4,000) as a means of draining the purses of rich industrialists who amassed great wealth while the rest of the country suffered. Some members of Congress fought the legislation, claiming it was unconstitutional to use taxation as a means of class warfare. The US Supreme Court soon declared it so. The opposition remained vocal in 1913, when the issue was raised again—this time in the form of debate over a constitutional amendment that would legitimize the power of the government to collect income tax. Some state officials were especially resistant because they believed federalism allowed states alone to enjoy the fruits of taxing their citizens. Speaker of the Virginia House of Delegates, Richard E. Byrd, warned that a federal right to collect income taxes would invite intrusive government and contribute to a growing imperialism in the capital. He remarked, "A hand from Washington will be stretched out and placed upon every man's business; the eye of the Federal inspector will be in every man's counting house." Despite such rhetoric, the states passed the Sixteenth Amendment in 1913 without much furor, and the modern age of income tax collection began.

Almost immediately, the federal income tax became a target for criticisms like those launched by Byrd. Opponents argued its collection of data violated privacy rights, its forms and procedures were unnecessarily complicated, its progressive gradations struck against the ideal of equal treatment for all. These types of complaints have dogged the powers granted under the Sixteenth Amendment ever since. In 2003, Grover Norquist, the president of Americans for Tax Reform, and Larry P. Arnn, a scholar at the Claremont Institute for the Study of Statesmanship and Political Philosophy, posted a brief article on Claremont's website that endorsed repeal of the Sixteenth Amendment. After indicting the income tax as "absurdly complicated, inefficient and intrusive," they called for a return of separation of federal and state powers, suggesting, "Wouldn't it be better just to keep all that money in the states in the first place? The federal government collected more than $600 billion in personal incomes taxes in 1996—about half its total revenue—but it spent more than that on welfare, health, education, transportation and housing programs. All these matters properly should be left to the states."

Similarly, in the 2011 Republican presidential candidate race, Governor Rick Perry of Texas was targeted for his views on repealing the Sixteenth Amendment—views he supposedly espoused in his book *Fed Up!: Our Fight to Save America from Washington*. Perry did refer to repeal as an option, but his more prominent idea was to replace the income tax with a "Fair Tax" that would increase revenues on consumption, not earnings. Perry's assertion brings to light another aspect of the wider argument against a federal income tax—namely, how to make up lost returns for a government so deeply in debt. In *At Issue: Should the Federal Income Tax Be Eliminated?* a collection of expert commentators and pundits debate the merits of the federal power to tax income. Some enumerate reasons why they believe the income tax goes against the core principles that the original colonists and Founding Fathers championed. Others put forth their notions of what substitute revenue-raising schemes might be more equitable and efficient. A few even defend the right of the government to impose income taxes to fund the necessary costs of improving the country and keeping it safe. In all, the viewpoints herein address not only issues of national financing but also question the proper function of government, its relation to its citizenry, and the ethics on which America was founded.

1

The Federal Income Tax Does Not Pay for the Functions of Government

Alan Stang

A respected news writer and foreign correspondent, Alan Stang is most remembered as a radio talk show host, most recently with his "Sting of Stang" program on the Republic Broadcasting Network. He was a champion of conservative values and an ardent opponent of communism. He died in 2009.

The federal income tax was not designed to pay the expenses of Washington. Tariffs and duties provide the finances necessary to fund the functions of government. Since the advent of income tax, however, the government has learned to spend more money than it needs to. Additionally, as the government spends more, it has divorced currency from any sound backing in gold or silver. Such fiscal policy is dangerous because it leads to inflation. Thus, the government cleverly uses income taxes to rein in inflation by removing some purchasing power from citizens, who otherwise would spend more and more unsecured money and drive down the value of the dollar.

Tote that barge, lift that bale, and make sure you pay on time. April 15th approaches and my guess is that only a relative handful of Americans knows why we have the income tax. With rare exceptions, they will exclaim that we must have the income tax to "pay the expenses of the government." Of course the truth is exactly the opposite. The income tax has nothing to do with paying the expenses of the government.

First an obvious fact, something you already know. When was the country created? Pick a date. Many would pick July 4th, 1776, when the Continental Congress adopted the nation's birth certificate, the Declaration of Independence. Many others would pick the date of ratification of the Constitution. Let's arbitrarily use 1776.

Now, when did we get the income tax? Except for the temporary income tax during Lincoln's Communist War to Destroy the Union, there was no income tax in this country until 1913, when the U.S. Supreme Court upheld its validity in *Brushaber* [*v. Union Pacific Railroad* (1916)], 240 U.S. 1. Indeed, even then it did not affect more than a handful of our people.

As late as 1942, only 3% of our people paid income tax. Until that date, most people probably had heard of it, but they didn't pay it and had never seen the form. It didn't apply to them. Indeed, if you check the records, you will see that in 1941, when the reader may have already been alive, the federal government collected more in alcohol and tobacco taxes than it did in income tax. Remember "moonshine" and the "revenooers?"

The income tax finally did hit the people in a big way only in 1942, and then only because we were of course in the middle of the war Franklin Roosevelt had finally succeeded in tricking us into by arranging Pearl Harbor. Even so, the conspiratorial warmongers could put the tax over only by calling it the "Victory" tax, a "temporary" tax collected by withholding, which would be repealed as soon as we had won the war.

The Nation Has Always Been Able to Function Without an Income Tax

Question: Name for me a year, just one year, between 1776 and 1942, when the nation couldn't function because we had no income tax. Can't find one? Okay name a month, just one month, when the nation collapsed, couldn't pay its bills, because we had no income tax. How about a week?

If we don't need an income tax to pay for the federal government, why do we have one?

Indeed, remember that during all that time, we fought many wars. We won them all. Yes, we won World War II with the income tax because it was "temporary," not yet a permanent part of our lives, but mainly because we fought that war on behalf of Stalin. With the income tax we have not outright won a war since, from Korea to Iraq.

Remember, you knew all this. I am simply reminding you of something you already knew. So, if we didn't have an income tax, yet never collapsed, where did the federal government get the funds to pay for itself? Again, they came from alcohol and tobacco taxes.

They also came from tariffs, which made foreigners pay for the privilege of selling products here. And they came from other indirect taxes. These were enough to pay for the few powers the Constitution grants to the federal government. Did you know that one of the biggest problems in Congress before the turn of the Twentieth Century was what the newspapers called the "tariff monster?" So much tax money was pouring into the Treasury that Congress didn't know what to do with it.

So, if we don't need an income tax to pay for the federal government, why do we have one? In August, 1942, [economist] Meyer Jacobstein, of the Brookings Institution, testified to a Senate subcommittee that "it is necessary to mop up the excess purchasing power of the community . . . because of its effect on the price situation. . . ." There are also a couple of Ohio University economists, Richard Vedder and Lowell Gallaway, whose study showed that for every dollar of increased taxes, Congress increased spending $1.58. In other words, taxes cause spending.

The Danger of Taxing When Money Is Not Backed by Gold

Now, another question you know the answer to. When there was money (gold and silver) behind our currency, the government had to deposit in the treasury the appropriate amount of money, in grains or ounces, whenever it printed paper currency. In the same way, you must deposit the appropriate sum in your checking account before you write a check against it.

Why doesn't the government just print what it needs; bigger numbers on bigger pieces of paper? . . . The answer is that doing so would constitute hyperinflation.

U.S. currency used to say it was "redeemable" downtown at the bank. The bank would pay the amount of money printed on the face of the bill to the "bearer on demand." Even early Federal Reserve Notes said that. The only difference between your personal check and government currency is that your check names the person to be paid and the government currency does not. It paid the "bearer," whoever had it in his hand when he walked into the bank.

Now here comes the question. Since there no longer is any money behind our currency; since the government no longer need find and deposit rare gold or silver into its account in order to write a check against it; and since paper and ink are relatively limitless in supply—indeed, computer entries, today's "money," are utterly limitless—why does the government bother to tax at all? Why the audits, the penalties, the raids and seizures, the divorces and suicides?

Why doesn't the government just print what it needs; bigger numbers on bigger pieces of paper? Even easier, why not just boot up and click on ever bigger computer entries; then use those computer entries to pay the bills? This is what Meyer Jacobstein was talking about. The answer is that doing so would constitute hyperinflation, which would send prices to Alpha Centauri and destroy the dollar here.

That is what happened in the Weimar Republic in post-World War I Germany, where the process took two years. It is happening now in Zimbabwe. The reason it has taken so long to happen here is that the financial geniuses who run the conspiracy for world government run the unbacked printings and now the computer entries through the non-Federal non-Reserve System, which is brilliantly designed to confuse and conceal what is happening. Extra layers of obfuscation have since been added, including the CDO [collateralized debt obligation][1] and other alphabetical horrors. I have explained the process many times; no need to do so again here. But it is happening and when the train stops we shall be in Weimar.

Redistribution of the wealth by government is communism. Subsidizing and penalizing various industries by government is fascism.

The man with the answers is Beardsley Ruml. Ruml was a lifelong Rockefeller factotum. Rockefeller is the family David Rockefeller boasts in his *Memoirs* is part of a globalist conspiracy against the United States. Ruml was chairman of the New York Fed. It was he who devised World War II "temporary" withholding. It was originally named for him: the "Ruml pay-as-you-go plan."

In January, 1946, *American Affairs* published a speech by Beardsley Ruml. The title was, "Taxes for Revenue Are Obso-

---

1. A CDO is an asset-backed security that pays dividends to various investors based on what level of investment risk they occupy. If the security fails or declines, those at the highest levels get a return while those at the lowest levels do not. The failure of mortgage-backed CDOs played a significant role in the collapse of the subprime mortgage market that followed a downward tread beginning in 2007.

lete." In it, Ruml speaks of two remarkable changes: "the gaining of vast new experience in the management of central banks," and "the elimination, for domestic purposes, of the convertibility of the currency into gold."

Under the heading, "What Taxes Are Really For," Ruml listed three main purposes: "as an instrument of fiscal policy to help stabilize the purchasing power of the dollar"; to express public policy in the distribution of wealth and of income, as in the case of the progressive income tax and estate taxes"; to express public policy in subsidizing or in penalizing various industries and economic groups."

Avoiding Hyperinflation Through Taxation

Redistribution of the wealth by government is communism. Subsidizing and penalizing various industries by government is fascism. You are seeing such fascism right now in the government "bailout" of certain favored companies. For instance, the government saved Goldman Sachs but flushed Lehman Brothers. What about stabilizing the purchasing power of the dollar? Ruml says this by far is the most important reason for the income tax and other federal taxes, sometimes called "the avoidance of inflation."

The true purpose of the income tax, therefore, is to inhibit the inflationary effect of ravenous government spending.

Ruml explains that "federal taxation has much to do with inflation and deflation, with the prices which have to be paid for the things that are bought and sold. . . ." If people have "too much" purchasing power, prices will rise. ". . . This will mean that the dollar is worth less than it was before—that is inflation. . . .

"The dollars the government spends become purchasing power in the hands of the people who have received them.

The dollars the government takes by taxes cannot be spent by the people, and, therefore, these dollars can no longer be used to acquire the things that are available for sale. . . ." So this is what Meyer Jacobstein meant by "mopping up purchasing power."

The true purpose of the income tax, therefore, is to inhibit the inflationary effect of ravenous government spending. The income tax allows our rulers to juggle their fiscal balls in the air a bit longer, by offering a safety valve through which the inflationary pressure generated by that spending can more safely be released. The income tax does that by *transferring purchasing power from the people to the government.* Again, it has nothing at all to do with paying the government's bills. . . .

All right, now you know why you pay income tax. Are you not inspired? On April 15th, when you put your head on the block, you will do so happily, maybe even singing the national anthem, in the knowledge that you are doing your patriotic part to mop up, to fight inflation and save the dollar.

2

The Federal Income Tax Is Immoral

D. Michael Martindale

D. Michael Martindale is an author, screenwriter, and film-maker living in Utah.

Although income taxes now seem natural because they have been part of the American way of life for decades, they are unethical and should be abolished. Income taxes suppress growth and investment and drain family finances. They also, among other things, foster a culture of envy that makes most poor and middle-income citizens distrust the notion that wealth comes from hard work. The country needs a national sales tax to replace income tax. A consumption tax would encourage people to make wiser financial decisions and prompt them to save more money.

April is the month of income tax returns, and the month of complaining about income tax. (Last month [April 2011] was no exception.) Some have suggested the income tax deadline should accompany Election Day so we can vividly remember what our elected leaders are doing to us while we vote for them.

Personally, I don't think that's a bad idea, because I consider the income tax to be immoral. It should be abolished altogether.

Nine Reasons the Income Tax System Is Immoral

There are nine reasons I think income tax is immoral, or unethical, or a really bad idea—however you want to word it:

1. It requires that we report highly personal things to our government, which is a serious invasion of privacy.

2. It's a violation of the basic constitutional right of not being forced to witness against oneself.

3. It invites the life-destroying abuses that the IRS is infamous for.

4. It penalizes the very things we should be promoting. Everyone knows that taxing something has the effect of suppressing that thing. (That's the whole premise behind constantly raising cigarette taxes.) Well, income tax penalizes the earning of income and savings and financial responsibility that motivates people to build an estate we can leave to our heirs so they can be cared for when we're gone. It penalizes business investment by forcing businesses to amortize those outlays over years instead of expensing them when the money goes out.

5. Income tax fosters the culture of envy that says stick it to the rich, under the illusion that all rich people got that way by inheriting it, being lucky, or cheating to get it, instead of the skill, perseverence, and hard work that most rich people got rich by.

6. It sucks resources out of our economy with the huge expense of recording and preparing information for tax returns, while producing nothing of value.

7. Some argue (and I'm inclined to believe) that a large reason why our families have had to become two-income families just to survive is because of the drain

on family incomes that income tax is. (Remember, income tax isn't just at the federal level. Almost all states, and many communities also have it.)

8. It invites usage of the tax structure for social engineering, not just revenue generation, and as a libertarian, I consider forced social engineering based on the rather arrogant philosophies of a fraction of the society to be immoral. Not to mention a great deal of the social engineering is based on political agendas and rarely on sound wisdom (e.g. biofuel from corn).

9. It forces businesses to make choices based on what will ease their tax burden rather than on what will make them most productive. Our health care mess today is one example of this, because it all started with health care benefits at work as an attempt to get around extortionary income tax rates of the time.

A National Sales Tax Seems the Best Alternative

The living generation has been weened on income tax, so it seems as if that means of taxation is as natural as breathing air. But it wasn't always that way—income tax wasn't even constitutional until well into the 1900s.

Does anyone truly believe the flat tax will stay flat? Every Congress will be tempted to tinker with the flat tax until it becomes just as complicated and unwieldy as our current tax code is.

There is an alternate option for taxation which I consider to be much less of an evil than income tax.

The so-called flat tax sounds like a good idea, but in practical terms there is no such thing. First of all, anyone who runs a business cannot have a flat tax because businesses incur legitimate business expenses which need to be deducted from revenue, and that guarantees complicated and controversial ways of defining what a legitimate business expense is. (Remember, business expenses impact any private citizen who files a sole proprietor C schedule, not just big corporations.)

Second, does anyone truly believe the flat tax will stay flat? Every Congress will be tempted to tinker with the flat tax until it becomes just as complicated and unwieldy as our current tax code is. Even before we've implemented the flat tax, people are already wanting to make exceptions for charitable donations and mortgage interest.

Although not without its drawbacks—there are trade-offs to everything—I consider a national sales tax to be the best option of all those being seriously considered today, for the following reasons:

1. It doesn't penalize what we want to have more of: income, savings, financial security. People complain about how consumer-oriented our society is, so let's tax that instead of income and savings!

2. It's inherently progressive, because people with more money purchase more things and will therefore pay more tax.

3. Those who are within a designated poverty level can simply apply for a tax-exempt status (like charitable organizations already do) and not have to pay the tax at all.

4. The costly, oppressive, privacy-invading system of reporting income will evaporate.

5. The collection system already exists in this country with state and local sales taxes being levied virtually everywhere—including the mechanism of granting tax exempt status.

6. Citizens will be able to manage their tax burden by making budgeting choices on what they choose to buy or not to buy, instead of being told, "You can afford to pay this much" even when people most assuredly cannot afford it in many cases.

7. Businesses can make financially sound choices to build their productivity and revenue instead of tax-evading choices that may conflict with productivity.

8. The IRS will cease to be the frightening Gestapo-like entity it is in our allegedly free society, and citizens can breathe easier every spring.

9. Every one of the nine immoral aspects of income tax listed above will cease to exist.

It's Time for a Reboot

A flat income tax would be an incremental improvement (i.e., better than nothing), but I don't think anything less substantial than a total reboot of our taxation mentality, such as a national sales tax would be, is going to bring us true tax reform.

We'd need to pass a constitutional amendment to be able to levy a national sales tax. But that's what it took to make income tax constitutional in the first place. It can be done again.

3

Paying the Federal Income Tax Is a Civic Duty

Walter Rodgers

A former news correspondent with ABC and CNN, Walter Rodgers continues to provide news journalism to the Christian Science Monitor *and other outlets.*

Paying income taxes is a civic duty that keeps the nation moving forward. Everyone should feel proud of paying to support the nation; it is a rewarding virtue to give to the land that provides so many services that have made the country great. Even if some tax money is spent on disagreeable policies, one must respect the notion of compromise that defines American democracy and feel proud that tax money is ensuring the survival of that ideal.

It's early April [2008], which means these are the few days of the year when Americans of almost every political stripe unite in a perennial ritual: complaining about taxes.

Count me out. I'm happy to pay my fair share to the government. It's part of my patriotic duty—and it's a heckuva bargain.

Taxes Are Patriotic

"Taxes are what we pay for living in a civilized society." Those words are written in stone, so they must be true. They're there to read for anyone who bothers to look up as they stroll past those New Deal-era government buildings on Constitution Avenue in the nation's capital.

They are the words of former Supreme Court Justice Oliver Wendell Holmes, Jr. Now there was a man! A patriotic taxpayer, not one of those chest thumpers who paper their cars with chauvinistic bumper stickers and grumble about supporting the government of the country they profess to love.

Before ascending to the court, Holmes served his country during the Civil War in places with names that still raise goose bumps: The Peninsula Campaign, Balls Bluff, Antietam, and Fredericksburg, where he nearly lost his life. When he finally died in 1935, Justice Holmes gave his residuary estate to the government in gratitude!

Now there's a man who truly understood patriotism in all its complexities. One facet requires citizens to pay up on April 15 because taxes are what citizens pay for necessary services.

Giving One's Fair Share

Paying taxes is an exercise of civic virtue akin to supporting one's country in time of war. Paying taxes is a conjoined twin of voting. When my wife and I emerge from our polling place on Election Day, I feel patriotic and virtuous. I am keeping my bargain with the Founding Fathers, affirming the privilege of being an American. It is a right that has roots stretching back to Magna Carta in 1215.

There seems to be an inconsistency about people who insist on wearing flag pins in their lapels, but who grumble about paying taxes.

I feel the same about taxes, paying my fair share to the republic. It affirms I am willing to share the burdens of the government that protects me.

Federal income taxes are a terrific bargain in America. I like to tell my tax-grumbling friends about my last year in Israel, when the Knesset passed a new tax code that would've seized 70 percent of my income. When I lived in Berlin, my tax rate was 50 percent, and when I left England three years ago I was paying a 40 percent rate to support a gilded monarchy and a national healthcare system that did not function very well. The only place I ever lived overseas and did not have to pay more than token taxes was the Soviet Union. There you got what you paid for. Only Moscow had potable drinking water and it was dodgy during spring runoff.

There seems to be an inconsistency about people who insist on wearing flag pins in their lapels, but who grumble about paying taxes. My friends grouse about government as though they had minimal financial or moral obligation to support it. Are they not part of "We the people"?

Helping Others Who Have Helped America

I never calculated how much I paid in taxes over a working lifetime, but I began when I was picking blueberries in Maine in 1954, so it must have been a lot—an awful lot. I am rather proud of my contribution to the US Treasury over a half century. My Social Security taxes have helped soften the blow of old age for many of the World War II and Korean War veterans. I hope my federal income taxes made the lives of woefully underpaid schoolteachers just a little more comfortable, helping with their Medicare or Medicaid bills.

Sure, there are things I would rather not pay for. I am not keen about farm subsidies to huge agribusiness concerns that are already as rich as Croesus. But democracy is the art of compromise, and Andrew Jackson was correct when he said, "The wisdom of man never yet contrived a system of taxation that would operate with perfect equality." Yes, professional tax planning can lead to adroit tax evasion. But reluctance to pay one's fair share flouts "the better angels of our nature." Genuine patriots don't complain about their patriotic obligations.

And oh, by the way, the words carved in stone on that federal building are at 1111 Constitution Avenue. It's the headquarters of the Internal Revenue Service. Pay up and be grateful!

4

The Real "1 Percent"

Michael Tanner

Michael Tanner is a senior fellow at the Cato Institute, a libertarian public policy research organization. His field of inquiry focuses on governmental domestic policies such as health care and social security.

The richest Americans—the so-called 1 percent—are much maligned in public and have become the focus of government crusades to balance what many see as a skewed tax system that unfairly saps the poor and middle class. In reality, the wealth of the rich has declined during the recent recession, yet they still bear the highest percent of the nation's tax burden. Targeting those fortunate few who have made good on the American dream of prosperity should not be the basis of public tax policy.

So just who are those top 1 percent of Americans that we're all supposed to hate?

If you listen to President Obama, the protesters at Occupy Wall Street, and much of the media, it's obvious. They're either "trust-fund babies" who inherited their money, or greedy bankers and hedge-fund managers. Certainly, they haven't worked especially hard for their money. While the recession has thrown millions of Americans out of work, they've been getting even richer. Worse, they don't even pay their fair share in taxes: Millionaires and billionaires are paying a lower tax rate than their secretaries.

In reality, each of these stereotypes is wrong.

Roughly 80 percent of millionaires in America are the first generation of their family to be rich. They didn't inherit their wealth; they earned it. How? According to a recent survey of the top 1 percent of American earners, slightly less than 14 percent were involved in banking or finance.

Roughly a third were entrepreneurs or managers of nonfinancial businesses. Nearly 16 percent were doctors or other medical professionals.

Lawyers made up slightly more than 8 percent, and engineers, scientists and computer professionals another 6.6 percent.

Sports and entertainment figures—the folks flying in on their private jets to express solidarity with Occupy Wall Street—composed almost 2 percent.

By and large, the wealthy have worked hard for their money. NYU sociologist Dalton Conley says that "higher-income folks work more hours than lower-wage earners do."

Because so much of their income is tied up in investments, the recession has hit the rich especially hard. Much attention has been paid recently to a Congressional Budget Office study that showed incomes for the top 1 percent rose far faster from 1980 until 2007 than for the rest of us. But the nonpartisan Tax Foundation has found that since 2007, there has been a 39 percent *decline* in the number of American millionaires.

Overall, the rich pay an effective tax rate (after all deductions and exemptions) of roughly 24 percent. For all taxpayers as a group, the average effective tax rate is about 11 percent.

Among the "super-rich," the decline has been even sharper: The number of Americans earning more than $10 million a year has fallen by 55 percent. In fact, while in 2008 the top 1 percent earned 20 percent of all income here, that figure has declined to just 16 percent. Inequality in America is *declining*.

As for not paying their fair share, the top 1 percent pay 36.7 percent of all federal income taxes. Because, as noted above, they earn just 16 percent of all income, that certainly seems like *more* than a fair share.

Maybe Warren Buffett is paying a lower tax rate than his secretary, as he claims. But the comparison is misleading because Buffett's income comes mostly from capital gains, which were already taxed at their origin through the corporate-income tax.

Moreover, the Buffetts of the world are clearly an exception. Overall, the rich pay an effective tax rate (after all deductions and exemptions) of roughly 24 percent. For all taxpayers as a group, the average effective tax rate is about 11 percent.

Beyond taxes, the rich also pay in terms of private charity. Households with more than $1 million in income donated more than $150 billion to charity last year, roughly half of all US charitable donations. Greedy? It hardly seems so.

And let us not forget the fact that the rich provide the investment capital that funds ventures, creates jobs and spurs innovation. The money that the rich save and invest is the money that companies use to start or expand businesses, buy machinery and other physical capital and hire workers.

It has become fashionable to ridicule the idea of the rich as "job creators," but if the rich don't create jobs, who will? How many workers have been hired recently by the poor?

No doubt dishonest or unscrupulous businessmen have gotten rich by taking advantage of others. And few of us are likely to lose much sleep over the plight of the rich.

But shouldn't public policy be based on something more than class warfare, envy and stereotypes?

5

The US Government Should Adopt a Flat Tax System

Stephen M. Musco

Stephen M. Musco is a certified public accountant living in Florida.

America needs a flat tax system—one that levies the same percentage on nearly every American. This would eliminate tax code and tax jurisdiction confusion, and it would help limit abuse of the system. The way to keep this tax low is to eliminate wasteful government spending, cutting services that government should not provide or services that private industry can handle better.

The latest twist on implementing a "flat" tax is [former Republican presidential candidate] Herman Cain's "9-9-9" plan. He proposes to tax individuals 9 percent and corporations 9 percent and to institute a national sales tax of 9 percent.

Many Americans live in jurisdictions that already have a sales tax. Many live in jurisdictions that have both a sales tax and a state or local income tax.

We have so many taxing jurisdictions and tax types in this country it takes your breath away. That is why we need to approach simplification one step at a time.

We need to replace the current income tax system with a flat tax, perhaps 17 percent.

Stephen M. Musco, "Why We Need a Flat Tax," (Sarasota, Florida) *Herald-Tribune*, November 25, 2011. www.heraldtribune.com. Copyright © 2011 by Steve M. Musco. All rights reserved. Reproduced by permission.

The proposed 9 percent tax for corporations is not even worth talking about.

Because of technology and the ability to report every shareholder's portion of a corporation's earnings to the Internal Revenue Service, corporate taxation has become obsolete.

A new, flat tax needs to be objective. The word "fair" is hardly ever appropriate when discussing taxation because, to most people, "fair" is what affects their personal pocketbook.

Instituting an Objective Flat Tax

A flat tax would affect almost everyone the same. I say "almost everyone" because self-employed individuals have an advantage: Their gross income is determined before their taxable income is determined.

For example, a self-employed person may have gross income or receipts of $100,000 reported on 1099 forms. But after deducting travel, meals, office supplies, licenses and rent, the net may only be $60,000. This is the amount that is therefore taxable, just like W-2 income.

In other words, self-employed people get to choose the expenses used to reduce the gross income. This can get highly subjective and there is much abuse.

Most employed taxpayers pay based on the gross income on their W-2 forms. If we apply the same principles to both sets of taxpayers, the flat tax would be objective.

Our federal government has to re-examine mandates and the level of services that are now rendered.

A National Sales Tax Will Not Work

Proponents of the national sales tax say it is needed to capture the nontaxed income of the "underground" economy.

True, it would capture some of this income.

However, everyone else in the "above ground" economy would be taxed again.

Some states, such as New York and California, have both an income tax and a sales tax. A national sales tax would bring the total tax paid by these individuals up to 45 percent to 55 percent.

It is the height of stupidity to tax everyone with an additional tax in order to tax those individuals who now do not show up on the radar. Unfortunately, this is how many politically correct laws are developed: Hurt everyone for the minority.

Eliminate Wasteful Government Services

Meanwhile, our federal government has to re-examine mandates and the level of services that are now rendered. There is no justification for going into debt to provide a service unless that service is:

1. A needed service that only the federal government can perform.

2. It is an emergency.

Other than national defense and a medical epidemic, I cannot think of an emergency that exists enough to cause the federal government to go into debt in order to render a service.

In addition, the government should not render any service to individual Americans that a private provider could provide. The government has no profit motive and therefore has no reason to be efficient. Medicare is a perfect example. Seniors need some type of coverage to handle their increased medical needs as they get older. If there had been no Medicare, someone would have invented a private version of Medicare and also made a profit.

We need to scrap the present tax system and replace it with an objective flat tax. The federal government must get out of the service business and budget for a surplus. Those are the only ways we can pay off the cumulative deficits of the last 50 years.

6

The US Government Should Not Adopt a Flat Tax System

Michael Chester

Michael Chester is retired from the field of industrial technology, in which he designed, built, installed, and repaired industrial manufacturing machinery.

Every so often, Republican presidential candidates push for a flax income tax plan as part of their campaign. They tout the tax as fair because it supposedly would be impartial and tax everyone at the same rate. However, a flat tax would certainly harm people with lower or middle incomes more than it would the very wealthy. That is, a person making lots of money would not have his or her personal purchasing power reduced very much compared to the significant drop in discretionary cash available to those in lower income brackets. America needs a fairer tax system, not just a simpler one.

With the actual Presidential election more than a year away, it is now the trial, error and silly season for the candidates. This is the time when candidates try floating new ideas and recycling old ones to see the reaction of the potential voters.

With there being no apparent challengers to Barak Obama in the Democratic Party, he is already in general election mode.

In the land of misfit politicians, AKA the Republican Party, they are dragging out all of the old reliable issues, both real and made up. One of these perennial decoys is the so called "Flat Tax." They try rolling it out every few years to muddy the waters. According to this myth, all income would be taxed at a lower flat rate than currently collected and the losses would be made up in volume. Everyone would pay the same rate and tax preparation would be greatly simplified. All sorts of rates have been proposed and all would benefit the wealthy at the expense of the poor and middle class.

The Flaws of Cain's Tax Plan

Herman Cain was the first to propose his "9-9-9 tax plan." Under his proposal, individuals and corporations would pay a flat rate tax of 9% and a Federal sales tax of 9% would be added. On the surface, this sounds fair, after all everyone would pay the same. Unfortunately, Michelle Bachman's speechwriter got it right. In one of the GOP debates, she was told to use the clever quip that if you turned 999 upside down, you would get 666 and the devil is in the details. (I am not criticizing her specifically for that; all political candidates are given clever "ad libs" to say by writers. She has plenty to criticize, but that is for a different time.) I hate using anything she says, but in this one case, she got it right. *Even a broken clock is right twice a day.*

Let's examine this plan starting with the 9% sales tax. Sales taxes are very regressive in that they affect people at the lower economic levels proportionally harder. Everyone has to buy basic products and services and the addition of 9% to their cost would price many basic essentials out of range. As an example if I buy a new $30,000 car under the current tax laws, I pay the 6% Michigan sales tax on it or $1800. Cain's additional 9% Federal sales tax would add another $2700 for a total of $4500 in sales taxes. If I borrowed the money for 4 years at 4% interest, the additional $2700 would cost me an extra $63.22 per month and an additional $234.68 in interest over the course of the loan. I might just decide that I really did not need a new car. Add this to the thousands of others who would come to the same conclusion and auto sales would plunge, auto workers would be laid off and be unable to purchase other products and those industries would lay off workers. Since these workers would not be earning wages, they would stop paying taxes and begin collecting unemployment insurance and the government would be in more debt.

As a percentage of income, [low-income people] pay the highest total tax rate.

The wealthy would purchase their big ticket items, such as yachts, overseas to avoid this sales tax and would put US yacht builders and their suppliers out of business. In the current fragile economy, these are the last things you would want to happen.

Companies Still Avoid Taxes Under Cain's Flat Tax Plan

The 9% corporate tax would greatly reduce government revenues. The current corporate rate is 35% but corporations are allowed to make deductions and get credits, so the effective rate is much lower. Last year General Electric actually had enough tax credits that the government paid them money for an effective negative tax rate. This was all within the law as they invested heavily in alternative energy and "green" technology which the government is encouraging through tax credits. They also benefited from provisions in the tax code put there for their benefit. At least in this case, some of this new technology may eventually benefit the country. Many businesses collect these benefits and do nothing for the general welfare of the country.

I have been told by people on the right that corporations don't pay any actual taxes because they pass those costs on to their customers. This is true as far as it goes, but that does not mean that they should not pay taxes. In my car example above, let's say that $1000 of the cost of my new car goes to pay GM's taxes. (I have no idea of the real figure, but I suspect it is much lower) If they paid no taxes, and passed along all of the savings, which is also highly doubtful, my new car would only cost $29,000 and the government would lose $1000 in revenue which everyone else would have to make up, so you all would be helping me buy my new car. True, your share of my car would be less than a penny, but multiply that by all the cars and other goods sold and it adds up to real money. Why should you subsidize my new car? You shouldn't. I get the benefits of the new car and I should be the one to pay for it. Cain's plan is light on details, but he does not say that he would get rid of corporate deductions, so most companies would pay little or no taxes.

Flat Tax Hurts the Consumer Classes

Now we get to the 9% personal rate. People with low incomes currently do not pay any income taxes, and that presumably would stay the same under his plan. Low income people do, however, pay payroll taxes, property taxes and sales taxes, so even though they pay no income taxes, they are far from tax exempt. As a percentage of income, they pay the highest total tax rate.

Now let's run some real numbers. A person working for minimum wage, $7.25 per hour, for 40 hours per week, for 52 weeks per year with no days off would earn $15,080 per year before any deductions. Taking out the employee contribution to social security at 6.2%, a total of $935, leaves this person $14,145 for the year. This person would probably pay no income tax. For the purpose of this example, we will figure that this person pays $500 per month in rent and another $500 for other essentials including food, clothing, insurance, etc. These items would be taxable under Cain's plan.

Necessities would total $1,000 per month, $12,000 per year, leaving this person with $2,145 to be spent on non-necessities. Remember that $6,000 is spent on taxable necessities. Using Cain's sales tax rate of 9% means that the person making minimum wage will pay $540 in taxes. Of the $2,145 that someone working 40 hours per week, 52 weeks per year, has left to spend, $540 of it goes to taxes, for a tax rate of 25% on their income after necessities are paid.

The bottom line [under a flat tax] is the minimum wage earner would pay an effective tax rate approximately 3 times that of the millionaire and the median income person would pay nearly twice the rate. This is in no way flat or fair.

Now let's figure taxes on someone making $1,000,000 per year. Taking out social security at 6.2%, should result in payroll taxes of $62,000, but the Social Security administration caps taxable income at $106,800 per year. So a person making $1,000,000 per year only pays $6,622 in social security taxes per year, for a rate of .6622% while the person making minimum wage pays 6.2%. The million dollar a year person will probably spend a lot more on necessities so we will figure $15,080 per month which is equal to a full year's gross at minimum wage. Therefore the person making $1,000,000 per year, paying $6,622 for social security, and $180,960 for necessities, is left with $812,418. From this we must take taxes at 9% of $90,480, half of what was spent on necessities. This yields taxes of $8,143 for the year for a rate of 1%. This is the result of the 9% sales tax. Now the millionaire would also pay 9% income tax after deductions. I will be very conservative and figure a 10% deduction for a taxable income of $900,000.

I am sure they could do better than that. 9% of $900,000 is $81,000 + $8,143 from above for a total tax of $89,143 or a final rate of 8.9%.

According to the US census, the average median income of employees in all states in the US is $51,575. Doing the same calculations for this person yields a tax of $7915 for an effective rate of 15.3%.

The bottom line then is the minimum wage earner would pay an effective tax rate approximately 3 times that of the millionaire and the median income person would pay nearly twice the rate. This is in no way flat or fair.

Fairer, Not Simpler, Tax Reform

Rick Perry and Mitt Romney have both recently come out with their own versions of the flat tax. The exact figures for their plans will calculate out differently, but the net result will be the same. Perry's plan even goes farther. He would completely eliminate capital gains taxes and all inheritance taxes. Most of the truly wealthy derive most of their income from capital gains (which are currently at the low rate of 15%, rather than the maximum rate of 35% on wages) on investments, rather than wages, so they would end up paying virtually nothing. A lot of people have been duped into believing that when old Aunt Betsy dies and leaves them $2000, the government will take most of it. This is a big lie told by people like the Koch Brothers [David Koch and Charles Koch, two industrialists who advocate lower corporate taxes] and the other Koch suckers to the Tea party and their followers. The truth is that aunt Betsy could leave you $20,000 or $200,000 or $999,999 and you would pay no Federal inheritance taxes.

The President has proposed raising the top rate to 39% on only the portion of a person's income that is over $250,000 and closing some glaring loopholes and, thus far, Congress has resisted. The party line at the GOP is that rich people need their money to create jobs. This is basically a steaming pile of bovine scat. The President's plan to give targeted tax cuts to those who create jobs is better than just giving them the tax cuts with no strings attached and hoping that they will create jobs, but not by much. People don't hire people based on tax cuts. They hire people when they have jobs for them to do. This means that they are selling their products or services and need more help to keep up with demand. The targeted tax cut might make a slight difference, if an employer is "sitting right on the fence" about whether to hire someone or not, but otherwise it would make no difference.

Most people believe that real tax reform is needed, but we need to make sure that we are getting something better and fairer, not just simpler.

7

The US Government Should Adopt a Consumption Tax System

Robert H. Frank

An economics professor at Cornell University, Robert H. Frank writes about the economy in a column for The New York Times. *He has written several books on the subject, including* The Darwin Economy: Liberty, Competition, and the Common Good.

To institute a fair tax policy, the government should adopt a progressive tax on consumption. By taxing only what an individual or family consumes, the country will learn some good habits. It will encourage savings and discourage wasteful spending. A consumption tax may also lead to other valuable social engineering if the country implements taxes on pollution, car weight, and other excesses that have harmful impacts on everyone's quality of life. In the short term, the planned implementation of a consumption tax would even lead to a spurt of buying as consumers rush to purchase luxuries before the tax takes effect. The spending spree could be just what the nation needs to pull itself out of recession.

Rising income inequality has been largely a consequence of two forces: changes in technology that have extended the reach of the most gifted performers in every arena, and increasingly open competition for the services of those performers. Finger wagging at corporate pay boards will not alter the strength of those forces. Regulatory reforms aimed at promoting better corporate governance are often desirable in their own right, especially in the financial services industry. But such reforms are also unlikely to alter the income growth trends we've seen in recent decades.

The good news is that we could pull a few simple policy levers that would greatly reduce the adverse effects of growing income gaps without threatening the benefits that have been made possible by improved technology and increased competition.

Determining Personal Consumption

The simplest step would be to scrap the current progressive income tax in favor of a much more steeply progressive tax on each household's consumption. Families would report their taxable income to the IRS (ideally under a tax code that greatly simplifies the calculation of taxable income), and also their annual savings, as many now do for IRAs and other tax-exempt retirement accounts. The difference between those two numbers—income minus savings—is the family's annual consumption expenditure. That amount, less a large standard deduction—say, $30,000 for a family of four—is the family's taxable consumption. Rates would start low and would then rise much more steeply than those under the current income tax.

Families in the bottom half of the spending distribution would pay lower or no higher taxes than under the current system. But high marginal rates on top spenders would not only generate more revenue than the current system, but would also reshape spending patterns in ways that would benefit people up and down the income ladder.

If top marginal income tax rates are set too high, they discourage productive economic activity. In the limit, a top marginal income tax rate of 100 percent would mean that taxpayers would gain nothing from working harder or investing more. In contrast, a higher top marginal rate on consumption would actually encourage savings and investment. A top marginal consumption tax rate of 100 percent, for example, would simply mean that if a wealthy family spent an extra dollar, it would also owe an additional dollar of tax.

A progressive consumption tax would not cure all ills. Although it would reduce inequality in consumption spending, it would likely have the opposite effect on wealth inequality, since the rich could better take advantage of the savings exemption.

Fiscal Alchemy

That feature of the tax gives rise to what it would be no exaggeration to describe as fiscal alchemy. Consider, for example, how the tax would affect a wealthy family that had been planning a $2 million addition to its mansion. If it faced a marginal consumption tax rate of 100 percent, that addition would now cost $4 million—$2 million for the job itself, and another $2 million for the tax on it. Even the wealthy respond to price incentives. (That's why they live in smaller houses in New York than in Seattle.) So the tax would be a powerful incentive for this family to scale back its plans. It could build an addition half as big, for example, without spending more than it originally planned.

The fiscal magic occurs because other wealthy families who'd also planned additions to their mansions would respond in a similar way. And since no one denies that, beyond some point, it's relative, not absolute, mansion size that really matters, the smaller additions would serve just as well as if all had built larger ones.

The tax would have similar effects in other luxury domains. The amounts spent on multimillion-dollar coming-of-age parties would grow less quickly, as would the amounts spent on weddings, yachts, jewelry, and other items. And these changes would attenuate the expenditure cascades that have squeezed middle-class families.

Benefits of a Consumption Tax Plan

A progressive consumption tax would not cure all ills. Although it would reduce inequality in consumption spending, it would likely have the opposite effect on wealth inequality, since the rich could better take advantage of the savings exemption. Because the wealthy would die with larger estates than before, it would be important to maintain a strong estate tax as part of the system.

With the unemployment rate still near 9 percent, now would be an inopportune moment to implement a progressive consumption tax. But if we passed the tax into law and scheduled it for gradual phase-in only after the economy had again reached full employment, we'd achieve three goals at once.

First, by committing ourselves to a larger revenue stream in the future, we'd reassure those who worry, justifiably, that the government cannot forever spend more than it takes in. Second, by encouraging additional investment, we'd foster more rapid growth in productivity and income. Third, and most important, knowledge that the tax was coming would stimulate a burst of private spending that would help get the economy back on its feet. Anyone who was thinking about buying a bigger yacht or building a bigger mansion would rush to do so before the tax took effect.

Of course, that's hardly the best way to stimulate a depressed economy. Far better would be for the government to spend hundreds of billions of dollars on desperately overdue infrastructure repairs. But conservatives in Congress have consistently demonstrated their ability and willingness to block such measures.

In contrast, conservatives have always been responsive to proposals to tax consumption instead of income. They generally favor a flat tax, but because flat taxes would make inequality dramatically worse, they are unlikely ever to be adopted.

Many on the right are quick to denounce taxes on harmful activities as "social engineering." . . . But that's what virtually all laws do.

So a progressive consumption tax may be our only politically realistic hope for ending the downturn quickly and limiting the growth in consumption inequality that has made life so much more difficult for the 99 percent.

The Value of Taxing Activities That Should Be Discouraged

In my recent book, *The Darwin Economy*, I defend the claim that taxes on activities that cause undue harm to others could generate more than enough revenue to end our budget woes once and for all. The progressive consumption tax is such a tax. The wealthy family that builds a bigger mansion or stages a more lavish wedding celebration almost surely had no intention of harming others. But its actions nonetheless harm others, by shifting the frames of reference that shape what they must spend in those domains. The progressive consumption tax creates an incentive to take those external costs into account.

For exactly analogous reasons, we should tax congestion, noise, and pollution. We should tax passenger vehicles by weight. In contrast, our current system generates most of its revenue by taxing useful activities. The payroll tax, for example, discourages hiring. The income tax discourages savings. As every mature adult realizes, we have to tax something.

Every dollar we can raise by taxing activities that cause harm to others is a dollar less we must raise by taxing beneficial activities.

Many on the right are quick to denounce taxes on harmful activities as "social engineering"—which they usually define as using the tax code "to control our behavior, steer our choices, and change the way we live our lives." But that's what virtually all laws do. Stop signs are social engineering, as are prohibitions against theft and homicide. Laws restrict behavior because individuals often choose to behave in ways that cause harm to others. For someone who cares about personal liberty, discouraging harmful behavior by taxing it should be far less objectionable than prohibiting it outright.

Time to Act

As economists are fond of saying, there's no free lunch. An important exception to that rule, however, is that when existing arrangements are grossly wasteful, it's possible for everyone to have more of everything. We must not allow mindless anti-tax rhetoric to prevent us from implementing tax reforms that would create enormous benefits for citizens all along the income scale.

Growing income disparities, which are largely a consequence of market forces, have made it far more expensive for middle-income families to achieve many basic goals. The OWS [Occupy Wall Street] movement has performed an invaluable service by helping to focus public attention on this problem. Members of the movement have wisely refrained from making specific policy demands for the moment. But now that inequality has reached the top of the agenda, it's time to discuss what to do about it.

8

The US Government Should Not Adopt a Consumption Tax System

David Glenn Cox

David Glenn Cox is a liberal Democrat from Chicago. He regularly contributes his opinions on national politics to the OpEdNews.com forum.

The notion of a "fair" income tax system to raise revenue based on a national sales tax is ridiculous. Inflating the purchase price for food, homes, automobiles, and other modern necessities will only hurt the working and middle classes. The rich, who live off a fraction of their worth and hide the rest of their wealth in investments, would be able to survive a national consumption tax, which is why they are often the ones who back such an idiotic strategy.

We've all had dumb ideas in our past and I don't exempt myself from this. I once threw Gunk engine degreaser on the floor to degrease it. Just one thing, I forgot to turn off the pilot light on the water heater first. Dumb? Man, that was dumb. After I got the fire put out my boss asked me, "Did you learn anything today?" I slowly shook my head and humbly answered, "Yes, yes I did."

But my mistake was an error, not of comprehension but of not planning before acting. These are simple mistakes and we've all made them and usually they don't require the fire department to correct them. We lock our keys in the car or give our keys to the spouse and forget to get them back.

Taxes That Add Up

On a grander scope are the errors that our mothers once advised about, "Look before you leap" and "All that glitters is not gold." I pointed out my own errors here because I'm going to point out the error of others. There's errors and then there are mistakes and then there's just plain stupid.

I speak of none other than the so-called "Fair Tax." The mother of all dumb ideas, there are no errors of any consequence in the world today compared to the "Fair Tax." George W. Bush has the intellect of [social critic Noam] Chomsky and the oratory skills of [former British prime minister Winston] Churchill when compared to the "Fair Tax." But, don't you see? It's fair! No, it's not, it's a farce!

A tax plan where you pay a 27% federal sales tax on all retail purchases. Your paycheck will be free of all deductions except for health insurance and, of course, your state withholding but this bullsh**it bamboozle is a bait and switch scam.

Proponents lead you to believe your paycheck will be all yours, free and clear, but it's a lie and no, it won't. Nor will the 27% federal sales tax free you from any city, county or state sales taxes, which, here in Cobb County, Georgia, is 7% so we are up to 34% right off the bat.

$100.00 worth of groceries will cost $134.00, times 52 = $1768 in sales tax per year. Now, if you have a family, it's hard to get by on less than $150.00 a week so your, "Fair Tax" is $2,652 per year, when most American's only pay around $3,000 per year in federal tax now and that is deducted from your pay check. The "Fair Tax" will be deducted from your children, as well; you'll pay tax on the food they eat, not dollars you earn. The "Fair Tax" will not free you from property taxes, state taxes, liquor taxes and cigarette taxes, occupational taxes, license taxes, automobile taxes, ad nauseum.

Want to buy a new car? A $30,000 vehicle will be an additional $8,100 dollars, will that be cash or check? Or, would you like to finance the balance for five years, if so that will add another $400.00 a year in interest on the sales tax alone! Or ten grand for sales tax in five years. Yessiree sir, that's gonna create lots of automotive jobs. So, you take your new car to gas it up at the pump and, although we've deducted the Federal excise tax and replaced it with the "Fair Tax", we've also left in place the state tax and you're right, at $4.00 dollars a gallon, that's bad. But its "Fair." Remember, every time that the price of gasoline goes up so does your tax bill because that's "Fair."

When a man with $33 million dollars tells you he has a "Fair Tax" plan, who do you think that fairness applies to? You? Or him?

Now, with the current Real Estate slump as it is, maybe the "Fair Tax" can help us out! A $200,000 house note balloons to $254,000. Just think, you get to finance $54,000 in sales tax for 30 years at say 7% or over $100,000 in interest over the life of the loan and that's just on the sales tax. "Honey, call the movers!"

A Deceptive Name

The "Fair Tax" scheme was instigated by Representative John Linder of Georgia, a man who listed his own net assets at $33 million dollars. So when a man with $33 million dollars tells you he has a "Fair Tax" plan, who do you think that fairness applies to? You? Or him? Linder first proposed his plan as "Income tax reform" but it never caught on with the public so they took it back into the shop and retooled it as, "Fair." Everybody likes "Fair." How can you be against "Fair?"

Everybody likes hot showers, too, that's why the Nazis led their victims to showers. If the sign on the door had said "gas chamber," no one would go in! So they bill the rape of the working public as "Fair." If enacted, the "Fair Tax" would be the largest tax increase on working people in recorded human history. Mr. Linder believes that there shouldn't be any capital gains taxes because that's not "Fair." Or taxes on foreign investments, no taxes of any kind on investments as, you see, that's not "Fair."

What is "Fair" is you paying the taxes on every morsel of food that you put in your mouth or stick of gum or every pair of kid's shoes that you buy. Every dollar you earn goes down in value by 27% but the good news is! The "Fair Tax" will eliminate the IRS. That's right! According to Linder, the billions in federal revenue collected by the "Fair Tax" will magically find its way into the appropriate coffers. How that will work, Mr. Linder is a little sketchy about, but with his giant brain working like it is, I suppose we should just trust him, right?

But, what about the poor? How will those unable to make ends meet now handle a 27% sales tax? Why, we'll just issue rebates to the poor, Linder says confidently. But Mr. Linder? Isn't that what the IRS does now? Are we to turn the world on its head just to get right back to where we started?

We all make mistakes but when some conspire to cheat you, that's no error, that's a con.

Tough Questions

I should confess, I used to live in Linder's district when he was a state Senator and first hatched this colossal humbug. My computer was new and I was reveling in the novelty of the Internet. I would ask questions to stymie him because I didn't think that he could answer them. I asked, "If you add 27% to the purchase price of house and the home owner defaults on the loan, who takes the hit? Is the Mortgage Company liable for the unpaid taxes on the transaction? Are the taxes paid in a lump sum or is it handled in the escrow? Would the debtor still be liable for the tax debt? How would the banks resell a $200,000 house with a $54,000 tax loss on top of the purchase price? Would it then be $254,000 plus 27%?" I don't think Realtors would like this plan.

What will happen to the bond market when every Real Estate purchase is escalated by 27% in price? I don't think the bond market is going to like that very much. What will happen to interest rates when 27% of all available Real Estate capital is sucked out of the market to be paid in, "Fair" taxes? I don't think the stock market would like that very much, either. When the economy slows down, tax collection will slow as well, many states are facing this problem with sales taxes now. How will the "Fair Tax" address that, as costs will remain constant?

We all make mistakes but when some conspire to cheat you, that's no error, that's a con. When a man with $33 million in net assets devises a system where he pays less and you pay more, it's a scam, bunko, a crime. Not only does he not belong in Congress, I'm not so sure he should be allowed to run loose on the streets. Point blank, for those of you who use 100% of your income to just keep the wolf from the door, you will pay 27% tax on 100% of your income. We will then magically reimburse those of you who didn't have the money in the first place.

A Modern Medicine Show

Now, if you've got 33 million in net assets, you probably live on 5% percent of your income. So 5% of your income will be taxed at 27% and 95% of your income will be tax-free, and that's called "Fair." That's what is called the "Fair Tax" but it's a patent, medicine show huckster making fantastic promises that they could never keep and dodging any questions or responsibility for the societal side-effects. A snake oil promise and a tent revival sales pitch, a modern day rainmaker.

Instead, we should offer Mr. Linder first class accommodations on the classic split timber transport. Where his body will be gently massaged with a specially heated petroleum-based sealant and his skin covered in a soft and fluffy, all natural, poultry down.

That's the way you deal with a fraud that's called "Fair!"

9

The US Government Should Adopt a Single Progressive Income Tax

Rich McSheehy

An engineer who worked on infrared sensors at the Massachusetts Institute of Technology, Rich McSheehy is now trying his hand at writing both fiction and nonfiction books.

Although America has a progressive income tax—one that increases the tax rate as incomes rise—the average citizen is forced to pay other taxes, such as state sales taxes, gasoline taxes, and property taxes on the money that has already been taxed by the federal government. This scheme was concocted by the wealthy to shift the burden of government costs to the poor and middle class. What Americans need is a single progressive income tax that would finance both federal and state functions and replace all other forms of taxation. That way, citizens would keep more of their paychecks and thus provide the means to jumpstart the flagging national economy.

I expect that everyone would agree that in order for a country, state, or city to function it needs money. For millenia these entities have obtained money, and still do, via a variety of charges imposed on the people in these locales. We usually call these charges "taxes." Over the centuries many types of taxes have been created: income taxes, excise taxes, property taxes, estate taxes, road use taxes, automobile taxes, boat taxes, sales taxes, poll taxes, Social Security taxes, value added taxes, financial transaction taxes, capital gains taxes, and so forth. There seems to be a semi-infinite list of the different types of taxes. Why?

Indeed. Why do we need so many types of taxes? The fact is we don't. The reason we have all these different types of taxes is that governments generally become corrupt and one special interest group or another gains an upper hand and uses their power to shift the tax burden to another, less powerful group of people. After a few centuries of this process we are left with a rat's nest of taxes that manages to tax the same dollars over and over again, while other dollars never get taxed at all. There has never been a better demonstration of the power of special interests and oligarchs.

No Need for a Harmful National Sales Tax

The solution is a single tax that is fair for all people and raises sufficient money so that the country, state, or city can perform its functions appropriately. The answer is not the so-called "Fair Tax"—a deliberate and viciously deceptive misnomer if there ever was one. That miserable concept is in fact one of the most unfair tax concepts ever created. It is simply another example of how the wealthy oligarchs of this country try to impose their merciless will upon the average person. The "Fair Tax" is nothing more than a national sales tax. The problem with this is that it taxes everything you buy: bread, milk, clothing, newspapers, gasoline, medical care, school supplies—everything you need to live—at the same rate as it taxes the playthings of the extraordinarily wealthy—things like 10 carat diamonds, 100 foot yachts, thirty room mansions, and so forth. So what's wrong with that? The problem is that even the fabulously wealthy don't buy a lot of those items so these things don't produce a lot of tax revenue. Most of the budgetary needs of the cities and states have to be made up from the sales of bread and milk and so forth. In this way the poor and indigent, the vast numbers of people living paycheck to pay check, and the families struggling to just get by pay pretty much the same tax as the wealthiest billionaires on most days. It is, in fact, "The Unfair Tax."

Our entire system of commerce contains taxes upon money that has already been taxed at least once.

The fairest tax of all is the graduated income tax: it is a tax that taxes small incomes very lightly and massive incomes heavily. Those who can pay the most do so and those who cannot afford to pay anything don't pay anything. Beyond being extraordinarily fair, the graduated income tax has another potential: it can, by itself, pay all the expenses of the budget of a state, city, or country. And that is a very good thing.

Taxing Already-Taxed Money

Consider our present situation. You have a job and maybe you make $1,000 a month. You pay $100 income tax per month. Then you take your money and you go out and by gas for you car. Suppose you buy $10 worth of gas. You only really get $9 worth of gas because the other dollar is for the gasoline tax— and really, it's just a tax upon the money you have already paid an income tax upon! Then you go to the grocery store and buy food. Same thing. Then you buy clothes. Same thing—you pay taxes on money that has already been taxed. Then you get your property tax bill in the mail. You've already paid for your house (with money that was taxed) and now you have to pay a tax again based upon how much you paid for the house. Your money that was already taxed is being taxed again—and it will be taxed again next year, and the year after, and the year after. Indefinitely.

Our entire system of commerce contains taxes upon money that has already been taxed at least once. It is the poor and middle class who suffer the most from this system because, proportionally, they have a much larger tax burden than the wealthy who have written all sorts of income tax, and other tax exemptions, for themselves into law and then pay only a small percentage of their income for the necessities of life—after all, they don't worry about a sales tax on food because you can only eat so many hamburgers, even if you are a billionaire.

A Single Graduated Tax Is Needed

If the leadership of this country really wanted to give a boost to the economy they would scrap our present complex system of national, state, and local taxes and create a single, sole, nationally controlled graduated income tax—and then outlaw all other forms of taxation. The government would then distribute these tax dollars to various states and cities in a manner proportional to their population so they can perform their functions of government. Such a tax would be fair and useful for the common good.

But we will never do that because, despite the fact that we vote for senators and representatives, we live in an oligarchy. Even our now corrupt Supreme Court rules that wealthy, and inanimate, corporations have the same free speech rights as *living people*—a ruling that defies sanity but allows the wealthy owners of these corporations to drown out the voice of the individual citizen. We live in a society where lobbyists carry bags of money to our elected officials, and they, in turn, create legislation on demand—for a fee. We live in a society where the financial burden of paying for the expenses of the country is placed squarely upon the poor and the middle class while many of the most wealthy pay nothing—yes, nothing—in taxes. And our Congress likes it that way.

A single, fair, graduated income tax is all this nation needs to function. Furthermore, the lifting of all sales, excise, transaction, property and other taxes upon commerce would produce a gigantic stimulus for our economy. There is, however, only one problem with my dream of having only one truly fair tax for all.

It will never happen.

10

The US Government Should Not Punish Corporations for Using Tax Havens

Richard W. Rahn

Richard W. Rahn is a senior fellow at the Cato Institute, a free market public policy research organization, and a former board member of the Cayman Islands Monetary Authority, which regulates the world's largest offshore financial center.

Politicians who are eager to raise taxes on US corporations seeking tax havens abroad are wrongheaded. This move is part of a vindictive scheme to squeeze more money out of already overtaxed businesses. It is sound financial sense for companies to relocate to low-tax jurisdictions. If the government wants to bring capital back to the states, then it should reduce corporate gains taxes and other penalties for investment. Companies use profits to grow; more taxes only inhibit this growth and force American companies to do business elsewhere.

If the government suddenly said you would incur more onerous and expensive tax regulations and reporting requirements if you moved your business to a low-tax state such as Texas or Florida from a high-tax state such as New York or California, you would be justifiably outraged. Now substitute Switzerland and Bermuda for Texas and Florida, and France and Germany for New York and California, and you'll understand a new form of "tax protectionism" that is infecting Washington.

Several serious proposals are being floated in the nation's capital that would penalize Americans for investing in low-tax rather than high-tax jurisdictions. Proponents say the measures are needed to catch tax cheats—but ignore the fact that most of the low-tax jurisdictions such as the Cayman Islands, Switzerland, etc., already have tax information exchange (for cases of probable cause), or tax withholding, agreements with the U.S. and other countries such as the U.K. and France.

Nevertheless, Sens. Carl Levin (D., Mich.), Byron Dorgan (D., N.D.), and Max Baucus (D., Mont.), as well as officials of the [Barack] Obama Treasury, want to make it more onerous and costly for American companies to do business around the world and for Americans to invest elsewhere. They would even make it more difficult for non-Americans to invest in the U.S.

To the extent tax competition between jurisdictions holds down the increase in the growth of governments, citizens of all countries experience more job opportunities and higher standards of living.

Looking for Ways to Wring More Taxes Out of Corporations

Mr. Levin's bill is a hodgepodge of tax increases, more regulations and penalties on American taxpayers doing business in targeted low-tax jurisdictions. Mr. Dorgan's bill would prevent certain American companies that operate and are incorporated outside the U.S. from being treated as nondomestic corporations, thus denying them the right of tax deferral until their income is brought back to the U.S. Mr. Baucus, chairman of the Senate Finance Committee, is circulating a draft bill that, among other things, would extend the statute of limitations from three to six years for tax returns reporting international transactions. The Treasury Department is proposing expanded regulations on foreign financial institutions that bring needed investment funds into the U.S.

In addition to charges of tax evasion, some members of Congress—echoing European politicians including France's President Nicolas Sarkozy and British Prime Minister Gordon Brown—have even tried to scapegoat the low-tax jurisdictions as somehow being responsible for the global recession. They are demanding that the G-20 [a coalition of twenty of the most economically developed nations] countries come up with action proposals against them at their meeting next month [in April 2009].

More Taxes Inhibit Growth

This is nonsense. The so-called tax havens are for the most part no more than way-stations to temporarily collect savings from around the world until they are invested in productive projects, such as building a new shopping center or semiconductor plant in the U.S. This enables a better allocation of world capital, leading to higher, not lower, global growth rates.

Indeed, to the extent tax competition between jurisdictions holds down the increase in the growth of governments, citizens of all countries experience more job opportunities and higher standards of living. And to the extent that businesses and individuals are discouraged by taxes or regulations from investing outside their own jurisdictions, they may simply choose to work and save less, period.

Those who demand increased taxes on global capital often rail against financial privacy and bank secrecy—forgetting they are necessary for civil society. It is true that not all people are saintly. But it is also true that not all governments are free from tyranny and corruption, and not all people are fully protected against criminal elements, even within their own governments. Without some jurisdictions in the world enforcing reasonable rights of financial privacy, those living in un-free and corrupt jurisdictions would have no place to protect their financial assets from kidnappers, extortionists, blackmailers and assorted government and nongovernment thugs.

It is a fool's errand to pass ever more laws against things that are already illegal, or to pass laws against people trying to protect themselves from rapacious and corrupt governments. Despite the hundreds of local, state and federal laws against financial fraud, and financial regulatory authorities like the SEC [Securities and Exchange Commission], Bernie Madoff was able to conduct the biggest ever Ponzi scheme for decades [in which he billed thousands of clients through falsified investment schemes].

The chief tax writer in Congress, House Ways and Means Committee Chairman Charles Rangel, Treasury Secretary Timothy Geithner, and former Senate Majority Leader Tom Daschle apparently did not report all of their foreign-source income. Their actions tell us that either the tax law is too complex, or they thought the tax burden was excessive. Would their behavior and that of millions of others improve by making the tax law more complex and punitive?

Driving U.S. Investments and Companies Elsewhere

U.S. companies are being forced to move elsewhere to remain internationally competitive because we have one of the world's highest corporate tax rates. And many economists, including Nobel Laureate Robert Lucas, have argued that the single best thing we can do to improve economic performance and job creation is to eliminate multiple taxes on capital gains, interest and dividends. Income is already taxed once, before it is invested, whether here or abroad; taxing it a second time as a capital gain only discourages investment and growth.

In fact, the U.S. does not tax most of the dividend, interest and capital gains' earnings of foreign investors in the U.S.— which means, ironically, that the U.S. is the world's largest "tax haven" for non-U.S. citizens, and that we benefit from hundreds of billions of dollars of needed capital invested here. If the U.S. did not treat foreign investors better than its own citizens (who are double-taxed on most capital income), most of the "tax avoidance" problems critics complain about would disappear.

The proposals by Messrs. Dorgan, Levin, Baucus and the Treasury will almost certainly have the unintended consequences of driving more U.S. businesses elsewhere, discouraging foreign investment in the U.S., and actually encouraging more U.S. investors to move their funds (either legally or illegally) not only out of the country, but to places in Asia or the Mideast that tend to be less cooperative with U.S. tax authorities than are the European and British low-tax jurisdictions.

The correct policy for the United States to follow is to reduce its corporate tax rate to make it internationally competitive, and to move toward a tax system that does not punish savings and productive investment so severely. We know from the experiences of many countries that reducing tax rates and simplifying the tax code improve both tax compliance and economic growth. Tax protectionism should be rejected because it is at least as destructive to economic growth and job creation as are tariffs on goods and services.

11

The US Government Should Eliminate State Corporate Income Taxes

Josh Barro

Josh Barro is a senior fellow at the Manhattan Institute, a free market economic policy research center.

Currently, the federal government, the states, and local munici-palities levy taxes on corporations. Because this system encourages states to woo corporations by lowering tax rates, and it compels the companies to make decisions based on tax laws and not other factors, the federal government should do away with state and local corporate taxes. Instead, the government should levy a single corporate tax that would be shared with the states based on block grants. These grants would never decline (even if the federal government had to run a deficit), so state revenues should remain stable. A new system would cut compliance costs, reduce tax burdens on corporations to spark growth, and sim-plify the tax code.

Corporate tax reform is hot in Washington right now. President [Barack] Obama called in his State of the Union for a revenue-neutral corporate tax reform that would lower tax rates—since a recent tax cut in Japan, the United States now has the highest corporate income tax rate in the OECD [Organisation for Economic Co-operation and Development]—

while closing loopholes and broadening the tax base. The House Ways and Means Committee held the first of what are likely to be several hearings on the matter last month [January 2011].

But if discussions of corporate tax reform focus solely on the federal tax code, we will miss an opportunity: the chance to abolish state and local corporate income taxes. Instead of focusing on lowering the federal rate, Congress should broaden the federal corporate income tax base and then forbid states and localities to tax corporate income—replacing their foregone revenues with an unrestricted federal block grant.

Difficulties in Complying with the Tax Code

Currently, states and localities collect about 14.7 percent of all corporate income tax in the United States in a typical year. (Local corporate income tax is rare; notably, New York City levies one.) Yet, because of a lack of uniformity in tax law and the complications associated with apportioning corporate income among states, state and local taxes account for about 30 percent of large companies' income tax compliance costs.

But more important than direct compliance costs are the economic distortions caused by state corporate income tax. Multistate corporations have significant leeway to determine the jurisdiction in which their income will be taxed—whether by actually moving operations or through accounting shifts—which had led states to enact beggar-thy-neighbor tax policies aimed at luring the most mobile firms to change states. When firms make business decisions designed to maximize tax advantages instead of pre-tax profits, the result is economic loss.

Meanwhile, in the last several decades, state corporate income tax revenue has dropped significantly as a share of the economy. David Brunori, a left-of-center tax law professor at George Washington University, characterizes the state corporate income tax as a "nuisance tax" and favors repeal. He says:

"It does not work for a variety of reasons, and the primary reason is ... state competition." Essentially, states have competed to sharply narrow their tax bases, and the state corporate tax has become more trouble than it's worth.

Conversion to a federal block grant would ... make it possible to address one of the key drawbacks of corporate income tax as a government funding source: volatility.

Of course, the 44 states that do tax corporate income are reluctant to repeal their taxes, as the taxes still do generate some revenue. Only the federal government has the power to wipe away this patchwork of nuisance taxes with a blanket prohibition on states levying them.

Advantages of a Combined State and Federal Corporate Tax

What would a world without state corporate income tax look like? It doesn't have to mean taking a crippling bite out of state revenues. By expanding the federal tax base and offering an unrestricted grant to state governments, the federal government can replace states' revenue loss. Even if structured in a revenue-neutral manner, this reform would improve the economy for two reasons: the combined federal-state corporate income tax rate would be lower, and federal corporate income tax is more economically efficient than state corporate income tax.

Conversion to a federal block grant would also make it possible to address one of the key drawbacks of corporate income tax as a government funding source: volatility. For example, state corporate income tax receipts were 17 percent lower in 2008 than 2007, according to Bureau of Economic Analysis data. While the federal government can run deficits to adjust for the effects of volatile revenues, states are forced to take painful fiscal adjustments when revenues fall sharply.

The federal grant should aim to replace the approximately 14.7 percent share of corporate tax revenue that goes to states under the current system. (That's the average figure from 1999 to 2008). But to avoid volatility, the grant should be smoothed based on a revenue trendline from the previous ten years, instead of equaling 14.7 percent of actual corporate tax revenues in the current year.

As an example, based on performance from 1999 to 2008, expected corporate tax revenues at all levels of government in 2009 were $412 billion, implying a state and local share of $60 billion. But due to the recession, actual revenues were just $232 billion. Under my plan, states would receive that $60 billion payment from the federal government anyway; conversely, when corporate profits are rising sharply, states could expect to receive less than 14.7 percent of actual receipts. Effectively, this would mean the creation of a new (though not especially large) automatic stabilizer.

A System That Would Work

There are some issues that would arise with a move to federal-only corporate income tax. One is the question of how to apportion grant funds among the states. Simply apportioning the receipts on a per-capita basis would transfer funds from rich states to poor states (as all major federal taxes do now.) Apportioning the funds in proportion to state GDP [gross domestic product] would reduce these transfers, though not eliminate them, as corporate profits make up a different share of GDP in different states.

It's also important to note that a reform that is revenue neutral nationally would not be revenue neutral for each state. States that currently place little reliance on the corporate income tax (or do not levy one at all) would get a revenue boost, while states with heavy reliance on such taxes would need to close a shortfall. In most cases, these effects would be small, as corporate income tax accounts for less than five percent of state and local government receipts. But some small states (notably, New Hampshire and Alaska) would need to levy significant new taxes to replace the substantial corporate income taxes they levy today.

Some conservatives might object that interstate tax competition is a good thing, and that the federal government would undermine it by effectively levying a uniform state corporate income tax. But in this instance, interstate competition has mostly led to the granting of special favors and the narrowing of tax bases—not a desirable form of competition. States would continue to compete and differentiate themselves on major taxes, especially those on personal income, sales and property.

Abolishing state and local corporate income tax looks like a bold step, but it is preferable to simply reforming the federal corporate income tax. My proposal would achieve all the same goals as a revenue-neutral federal corporate tax reform, while also reducing compliance costs and doing more to reduce the economic burden of corporate taxation. And with a consensus in Washington that corporate tax reform is needed, abolishing these taxes may be more feasible than ever.

12

The US Government Should Eliminate All Taxes

Bob Adelmann

Bob Adelmann is a libertarian writer who contributes to the New American *and regularly wrote for the now-defunct* Constitutionalist Today *conservative newspaper.*

As Congress debates ways to adjust income tax rates to meet the needs of government, a few things are clear. Neither the flat tax nor fair tax proposals will meet with success. Both fail to recognize that taxes should not be dependent on the voraciousness of government spending. The answer is to rein in government and pare it back down to its constitutionally mandated services. In this manner, the country will have the revenue to pay for the needs of government; it just will not need more money to pay for government waste. Therefore, the debate should not be about which tax plan is best suited to the country. No tax plan is warranted under the Constitution, and all income taxes should be eliminated.

Stephen Moore's math in his [May 26, 2011] *Wall Street Journal* article is compelling: by the time the Democrats' proposed three-percent surtax on incomes over $1 million a year is added to all the other taxes people pay, those at the high end would be paying 62 percent of their income in federal and state income taxes.

He adds together the current 35 percent top income tax bracket to the three percent surtax, along with the expected repeal of the [George W.] Bush "tax cuts" in 2012, payroll taxes, Social Security and Medicare taxes, the 0.9 percent Medicare surtax, the hidden 3.8 percent sales tax in ObamaCare which begins in 2014, and state income taxes, and he comes out, inevitably, to 62 percent on the highest income earners.

What's particularly distressing to Moore is the massive change this represents over just the past 20 years. In 1990, the highest individual income tax rate in the United States was 33 percent while the average of the country's trading partners was 51 percent. He says, "No wonder that during the 1980's and 90's the U.S. created *more than twice as many new jobs as Japan and Western Europe combined.*" (Emphasis added.) He adds,

> What all this means is that in the late 1980's, the U.S. was nearly the lowest taxed nation in the world, and a quarter century later we're nearly the highest.

Moore's solution? "If there were ever a right time to trade in the junk heap of our federal tax code for a pro-growth [business publishing executive] Steve Forbes-style flat tax, now's the time."

Flat Tax Flaws

A flat tax, on the surface, looks attractive. It is estimated that the Internal Revenue Code contains some nine million words, and is full of loopholes, deductions, and exemptions which make calculating and collecting taxes a costly labyrinthine nightmare. Some estimates put the cost of compliance at $350 billion a year; others are even higher. The code also has long been used to implement "social policy," which is a nice way of saying government sanctions to control people's behavior. A good example is the mortgage interest deduction to provide an incentive to encourage home ownership. And those loopholes, as [economics professor] Thomas DiLorenzo notes, come at a price: special interest lobbyists descending on Congress like locusts, seeking special dispensation for their specific industry or company.

Proponents [of the fair tax] claim many of the same benefits as a flat tax, including greatly reducing collection costs, broadening the tax base, and drawing in from the underground economy wealth that currently isn't being taxed.

A flat tax then, of perhaps 17 percent on income, wherever derived, would certainly appear to simplify the process. Proponents suggest that taxes could be calculated on a postcard in just a few minutes. The number of tax returns to be filed would drop precipitously, reducing the size and cost of the Internal Revenue Service significantly. And raising the tax rate in the future would be resisted because Congress would have great difficulty gaining the support of a significant majority of the populace, as each of them would feel the pain.

Opponents of a flat tax point out that even a small bite out of a low-income taxpayer would be disproportionately painful when compared to a higher-income taxpayer, and so some sort of "adjustments" to the flat tax—i.e., deductions or exemptions—would have to be made to make a flat tax "fair." And the moment that happens, of course, the flat tax is no longer flat, but progressive, with higher-income taxpayers bearing more of the burden, just as they do now. Others would remind proponents that a flat tax would leave in place Social Security and Medicare taxes.

Fair Tax Failures

As an alternative, the fair tax has been proposed, which would replace all federal taxes on income with a national sales tax. The tax rate suggested by Rep. John Linder (R-Ga., - retired) in 1999 and every year until his retirement in 2010 is 23 percent and would apply only once, at the point of purchase, on "all new goods and services for personal consumption."

Proponents claim many of the same benefits as a flat tax, including greatly reducing collection costs, broadening the tax base, and drawing in from the underground economy wealth that currently isn't being taxed (estimated by some to exceed $1 trillion annually). Built into the fair tax legislation is repeal of the 16th Amendment in order to prevent Congress from re-establishing another income tax in the future. The fair tax legislation would terminate the Internal Revenue Service after three years, and it would replace not only all federal income taxes (including corporate income taxes and the Alternative Minimum Tax), but also all payroll taxes, Social Security and Medicare taxes, gift taxes, and estate taxes.

Opponents of the fair tax doubt that the IRS would be abolished, and believe that getting the 16th Amendment abolished would require a Herculean effort, taking years to accomplish. They also point out that the legislation provides for a "pre-bate" from the government to offset the tax impact on basic necessities, thus putting every American on the dole.

Support in the Congress for Linder's fair tax bill has waxed and waned over the years, with just 56 cosponsors of the bill in 1999 and only 67 in the 112th Congress.

All the discussion about a flat tax or a fair tax ... deflects the conversation away from the only serious discussion that's worth having: reducing the size, reach, power, influence, impact, and cost of government itself.

The Problem with "Fair Share" Mentality

Regardless of the proposed plans to simplify and equalize the impact of the tax code, each suffers from the most grievous disadvantage: They are both "revenue neutral," which means simply that revenues to the federal government would remain the same as under the current system. In other words, all the discussion about how to collect taxes never includes any discussion about *the amount government is spending.* Discussions always assume that the federal government has a "right to confiscate a percentage" of every individual's wealth, either through a sales (or consumption) tax or an income tax. As Professor Murray Rothbard wrote, both of these taxes can only be regarded as a payment for permission-to-live. [They] imply that a man will not be allowed to advance or even sustain his life unless he pays, off the top, a fee to the State for permission to do so. . . .

What Republicans want is a slight reduction in the welfare state with an increase in the warfare state. Democrats regularly call for just the opposite: a slight reduction in the warfare state with an increase in the welfare state.

[These movements are] part of a process by which the government and its allies have been able to split and deflect the tax protest movement from trying to lower the taxes of everyone, into trying to force everyone into paying [their] "fair share."

In fact, all the discussion about a flat tax or a fair tax is just a waste of time and energy, and deflects the conversation away from the only serious discussion that's worth having: reducing the size, reach, power, influence, impact, *and cost* of government itself. As [libertarian author] Laurence Vance angrily noted in his talk to the Gulf Coast Economics Club in Pensacola, Florida, two weeks ago,

> All the proposals put forth by the Democratic and Republican parties to rein in government spending are nothing but band aids and window dressing: baseline budgeting, a Balanced Budget Amendment, automatic across-the-board spending cuts, sunset provisions, spending increases limited

to the rate of inflation, spending caps based on GDP [gross domestic product], deficit reduction targets, elimination of earmarks, deficit commissions, temporary freezes on certain categories of spending, rollbacks to some previous level, non-binding public voting on spending cuts, and, of course, cutting waste, fraud, abuse, and unnecessary spending.

What Republicans want is a slight reduction in the welfare state with an increase in the warfare state. Democrats regularly call for just the opposite: a slight reduction in the warfare state with an increase in the welfare state.

Limiting Government Is a Chief Part of the Tax Solution

A careful reading of Article 1, Section 8 of the Constitution reveals that only the Departments of State, Treasury, Justice, and Defense are provided for. Following the Constitution, then, would lead one to conclude that the following are not constitutional and should be abolished: the Federal Reserve, the Departments of Agriculture, Commerce, Education, Energy, Health and Human Services, Housing and Urban Development, Interior, Labor, and Transportation, along with a whole host of alphabet soup agencies including the DEA, the BATFE, the NEA, the SBA, the NLRB, FEMA, and OSHA.

By forcing the conversation toward these issues, attempts to deflect and distract (such as a flat tax or a fair tax) would be seen for what they are, and the real job of forcing government back into its constitutional bounds can begin. As Vance noted,

> Limiting government to its proper role will automatically cause the spending problem to disappear. The government needs to be gotten completely out of the places it doesn't belong. . . .

The income tax code doesn't need to be simplified, shortened, fairer, or less intrusive. And neither do the income tax rates need to be made lower, flatter, equal, or less progressive.

It should be remembered that the Republic operated for its first 125 years without an income tax. Instead of a flat tax or a fair tax, how does no tax sound?

Organizations to Contact

The editors have compiled the following list of organizations concerned with the issues debated in this book. The descriptions are derived from materials provided by the organizations. All have publications or information available for interested readers. The list was compiled on the date of publication of the present volume; the information provided here may change. Be aware that many organizations take several weeks or longer to respond to inquiries, so allow as much time as possible.

American Enterprise Institute (AEI)

1150 Seventeenth St. NW, Washington, DC   20036
(202) 862-5800 • fax: (202) 862-7177
website: www.aei.org

As a nonpartisan, public policy organization, the American Enterprise Institute (AEI) researches pertinent policy issues, presents its findings in publications for the public and policy makers to review, and suggests future policy directions. The organization generally supports income tax reform that does away with the current system, which the organization views as costly and complicated, and replaces it with a progressive consumption tax. Publications detailing AEI's views on this issue can be read on the organization's website in articles such as "Happy Birthday, America! Time to Totally Overhaul Your Tax Code," "A Simple Tax Code Is a Fair Tax Code," and "The Capital Gains Preference: Imperfect, but Useful."

Americans for Fair Taxation

PO Box 27487, Houston, TX   77227-7487
(713) 963-9023 • fax: (713) 963-8403
e-mail: info@fairtax.org
website: www.fairtax.org

Americans for Fair Taxation is a grassroots organization seeking to replace the current tax system with a national sales tax on new goods and services. The organization works to promote economic research, educate both citizens and community leaders, and mobilize grassroots efforts for change. Detailed reports on this tax proposal can be found on the group's website.

Americans for Tax Reform (ATR)
722 12th St. NW, Fourth Floor, Washington, DC   20005
(202) 785-0266 • fax: (202) 785-0261
e-mail: ideas@atr.org
website: www.atr.org

Americans for Tax Reform (ATR) has been working since 1985 to promote tax reform that simplifies taxes by making them flat, low, and visible and reduces the government's ability to control its citizens' lives through taxation. Information about the ATR federal tax reform plan is laid out on the organization's website, along with details about individual states' tax systems. Additional articles on spending and transparency, regulatory burden, and specific industry issues can be found on the Americans for Tax Reform website.

Brookings Institution
1775 Massachusetts Ave. NW, Washington, DC   20036
(202) 797-6000
website: www.brookings.edu

Brookings Institution is a Washington, DC-based public policy think tank that seeks to conduct independent research and offer policy recommendations to create a stronger American democracy; improve the economic and social welfare, security, and opportunity for American citizens; and create an open, prosperous and cooperative international system. While the organization views the current federal income tax system as an important source of revenue, it does recognize the complexity and inequality that can result due to this system. As such, the organization offers numerous suggestions for dealing with the current tax system, and in combination with the Urban Institute created the Tax Policy Center to tackle current tax reform issues. The site can be accessed at www.taxpolicy center.org.

Cato Institute

1000 Massachusetts Ave. NW, Washington, DC 20001-5403
(202) 842-0200 • fax: (202) 842-3490
website: www.cato.org

Cato Institute is a public policy organization that promotes the Libertarian ideals of limited government, free markets, individual liberty, and peace in US government policy. The Institute favors low taxes and reduced government spending. Cato reports on US tax policy have explored the different options for federal tax reform extensively and offer a range of recommendations on this issue. Articles such as "Tax-Spend or Fiscal Illusion?" "This Is Fair," and "Obama: Tax 'The Rich'" can be read on the Cato website and offer opinions on the current tax system and what can be done to change it.

Center for American Progress (CAP)

1333 H St. NW, 10th Floor, Washington, DC 20005
(202) 682-1611 • fax: (202) 682-1867
website: www.americanprogress.org

An independent, nonpartisan educational organization, the Center for American Progress (CAP) conducts research and publishes reports promoting progressive ideas and action with the desire to make the lives of all Americans better. The organization's work focuses on the development of new policy ideas, critiquing conservative based policy, pushing the media to cover significant issues, and framing the national debate on these topics. On tax policy issues, CAP favors progressive tax policy and opposes the implementation of a flat tax. Articles accessible on the organization's website, including "The Federal Tax Code and Income Inequality," "The Richest 1 Percent Get More, Pay Less," and "The Good Old Double Reverse," along with many others, comment on tax reform plans and offer alternative solutions.

The Heritage Foundation

214 Massachusetts Ave. NE, Washington, DC 20002-4999
(202) 546-4400 • fax: (202) 546-8328

e-mail: info@heritage.org
website: www.heritage.org

The Heritage Foundation is a public policy think tank that seeks to advance conservative ideals such as free enterprise, competition and individual responsibility, limited government, and a strong national defense in the government policies it promotes. With regard to tax policy, Heritage believes that the tax code must be reformed to encourage work, saving, investment, and entrepreneurship, and the best way to do this is with its plan the "New Flat Tax," under which both families and businesses would pay taxes under a single tax rate. Information detailing this plan, explaining the problems with the current tax system, and describing the steps to reform can be found on the Heritage website.

Internal Revenue Service (IRS)
1111 Constitution Ave. NW, Washington, DC   20224
(800) 829-1040
website: www.irs.gov

The Internal Revenue Service (IRS) is the tax administration bureau within the US Department of the Treasury that oversees the collection of all taxes from the US citizens and businesses. The IRS works to ensure that all individuals and corporations comply with US tax law and pay the taxes they owe to the government. Information about current tax codes for all entities within the country can be found on the IRS website.

Tax Foundation
National Press Bldg., 529 14th St. NW, Suite 420
Washington, DC   20045-1000
(202) 464-6200
e-mail: tf@taxfoundation.org
website: www.taxfoundation.org

The Tax Foundation has worked since its founding in 1937 to ensure that taxpayers are educated about sound tax policy and the tax burden placed on Americans; the organization views this knowledge as the basis of a free society. The Foundation's website is divided into federal, state, and legal reform sections with general information about taxes as well as a range of tax topics, including federal taxes, income taxes, and sales and use taxes, among others. Articles, blog posts, and videos offer accessible information about the US tax code and regulation.

Urban Institute (UI)
2100 M St. NW, Washington, DC 20037
(202) 833-7200
website: www.urban.org

The Urban Institute (UI) has been working since the 1960s to collect data, research policy issues, assess current government programs, and provide information to Americans concerning social and economic issues, with the goal of encouraging effective public policy and government. UI promotes tax reform that simplifies taxes while making them fairer and more efficient. Publications detailing the organization's suggestions can be found on its website, with more focused information available from the Tax Policy Center, a joint effort of UI and the Brookings Institution, which can be found at www.taxpolicy center.org.

US Chamber of Commerce
1615 H St. NW, Washington, DC 20062-2000
(202) 659-6000
website: www.uschamber.com

The US Chamber of Commerce is a nonprofit organization that serves as the voice of American business before the US Congress, government agencies, and the courts. The Chamber sees current US tax policy as stifling investment in American business and causing US business to fall behind in competition with international companies. The organization lays out a tax reform plan on its website that it believes would better benefit both American businesses and citizens. Information about this plan and other income tax issues can be found on the US Chamber of Commerce website.

US Department of the Treasury

1500 Pennsylvania Ave. NW, Washington, DC   20220
(202) 622-2000 • fax: (202) 622-6415
website: www.treasury.gov

The US Department of the Treasury is the government agency charged with ensuring the strength and stability of the US economy. While the agency's reach is wide with regard to economic policy, the Treasury website provides detailed information about various types of tax reform, goals, and framework currently under consideration.

Bibliography

Books

Bruce Bartlett — *The Benefit and the Burden: Tax Reform: Why We Need It and What It Will Take.* New York: Simon & Schuster, 2012.

Neal Boortz and John Linder — *The Fair Tax Book: Saying Goodbye to the Income Tax and the IRS.* New York: HarperCollins, 2005.

W. Elliot Brownlee — *Federal Taxation in America: A Short History.* New York: Cambridge University Press, 2004.

Leslie Carbone — *Slaying Leviathan: The Moral Case for Tax Reform.* Dulles, VA: Potomac, 2009.

John W. Diamond and George R. Zodrow, eds. — *Fundamental Tax Reform: Issues, Choices, and Implications.* Cambridge: Massachusetts Institute of Technology Press, 2008.

Steve Forbes — *Flat Tax Revolution: Using a Postcard to Abolish the IRS.* Washington, DC: Regnery, 2005.

Michael J. Graetz — *100 Million Unnecessary Returns: A Simple, Fair, and Competitive Tax Plan for the United States.* New Haven, CT: Yale University Press, 2008.

Robert E. Hall and Alvin Rabushka — *The Flat Tax*, 2nd ed. Stanford, CA: Hoover Institution, 2007.

Ken Hoagland — *The FairTax Solution: Financial Justice for All Americans*. New York: Penguin, 2010.

Edward J. McCaffery — *Fair Not Flat: How to Make the Tax System Better and Simpler*. Chicago: University of Chicago Press, 2002.

Rick Perry — *Fed Up!: Our Fight to Save America from Washington*. New York: Little Brown, 2010.

Joel Slemrod and John Bakija — *Taxing Ourselves: A Citizen's Guide to the Debate over Taxes*, 4th ed. Cambridge: Massachusetts Institute of Technology Press, 2008.

C. Eugene Steuerle — *Contemporary U.S. Tax Policy*, 2nd ed. Washington, DC: Urban Institute, 2008.

Martin A. Sullivan — *Corporate Tax Reform: Taxing Profits in the 21st Century*. New York: Apress, 2011.

Periodicals and Internet Sources

Confidence W. Amadi and Felicia Y. Amadi — "United States Tax Reform: A Common Sense Approach," *International Journal of Business & Management*, June 2012.

Tim Cavanaugh — "Fair Tax or Foul?" *Reason*, August/September 2011.

Nancy Cook   "Why a Flat Tax Could Lose Its
                    Luster," *National Journal*, October 29,
                    2011.

Mihir A. Desai   "A Better Way to Tax U.S.
                    Businesses," *Harvard Business Review*,
                    July/August 2012.

Gary Dorrien   "Occupy the Future," *America*, March
                    12, 2012. http://americamagazine.org.

Economist   "The Craze for Flat Taxes," October
                    29, 2011.

Steve Forbes   "Non-Flat Falls Flat," *Forbes*, April 11,
                    2011.

Philip Gulley   "Forms of Punishment," *Indianapolis
                    Monthly*, April 2012.

Kip Hagopian   "The Inequity of the Progressive
                    Income Tax," *Policy Review*,
                    April/May 2011.

Danny Heitman   "Tax Day: How to Remind
                    Americans That Paying Taxes Is a
                    Conservative Value," *Christian Science
                    Monitor*, April 17, 2012.

William P. Hoar   "Fair or Foul, Washington Wants
                    More," *New American*, March 5, 2012.

*International   "Can Tax Reform Save the U.S.
Economy*   Economy?" Winter 2012.

Jennifer Hope   "You Get What You Pay For,"
Kottler   *Sojourners Magazine*, April 2010.

Jillian Mack   "Abolish Income Taxes and Enact the 'Fair Tax': A Libertarian Viewpoint," *Dayton Daily News*, April 15, 2012.

Donald B. Marron   "Spending in Disguise," *National Affairs*, Summer 2011.

Susan Moore   "Heartburn from Paying Taxes? Then How about the Fair Tax?" *Inside Tucson Business*, May 4, 2012.

Adam H. Rosenzweig   "Why Are There Tax Havens?" *William & Mary Law Review*, December 2010.

Richard Rubin   "Fair Tax: A Simple Idea Full of Complications," *Bloomberg Businessweek*, April 11, 2011.

Richard Rubin and Peter Coy   "Rick Perry's Not-Really-All-That-Flat Tax," *Bloomberg Businessweek*, October 31, 2011.

Dennis J. Ventry Jr.   "Americans Don't Hate Taxes, They Hate Paying Taxes," *U.B.C. Law Review*, September 1, 2011.

Index

O

Obama, Barack, 27, 34, 59, 63
ObamaCare, 69
Occupy Wall Street (OWS), 27, 46
Ohio University, 13
The one percent, 27–29
Organisation for Economic Co-operation and Development (OECD), 63–64

P

Passenger vehicle tax, 45
Payroll taxes, 45, 69, 71
Perry, Rick, 9, 39
Poll tax, 54
Pollution tax, 45
Ponzi scheme, 61
Privacy rights, 8, 19, 21
Private charity, 29
Progressive income tax, 16
Property tax, 7, 37, 55
Purchasing power, 16–17

R

Rahn, Richard W., 58–62
Rangel, Charles, 61
Real Estate slump, 49
Recession, 27, 28, 60, 66
Republican Party, 35
Revenue neutral reform, 66
Rockefeller, David, 15
Rodgers, Walter, 23–26
Romney, Mitt, 39
Roosevelt, Franklin, 12
Rothbard, Murray, 72
Ruml, Beardsley, 15–16

S

Sales tax
  collection of, 21, 51
  existence of, 30, 32, 54
  interest on, 49
  low income and, 37
  rates of, 38, 48, 50, 69
  as regressive, 35–36
  See also National sales tax
Sarkozy, Nicolas, 60
Securities and Exchange Commission (SEC), 61
Self-employed persons, 31
Senate Finance Committee, 59
Single progressive income tax
  already-taxed money, 55–56
  government should adopt, 53–57
  national sales tax *vs.*, 54–55
  need for, 56–57
  overview, 53–54
Sixteenth Amendment, 8–9, 71
Social Security administration, 38
Social Security taxes, 25, 54, 69, 71
Soviet Union, 25
Stang, Alan, 11–17
State corporate income tax
  elimination benefits, 66–67
  federal corporate tax and, 65–66
  federal tax code compliance, 64–65
  government should eliminate, 63–67
  overview, 63–64
Stevens, Thaddeus, 7
The super-rich, 28
Switzerland, 58–59